"Cindy Shepard has been a contributor to my motivational Facebook group, *Intentions, Affirmations, and Manifestations*, almost since its inception. I, as well as the members of the group, eagerly look forward to her astute observations, clever insights, and powerful – often emotional – writing. She is one of our most-read columnists and her posts and contributions consistently generate extensive feedback and comments. I'm honored to have her as part of the team."

Scott 'Q' Marcus

Cynthia L. Shepard

Picking up the Pieces

MUSINGS ON CHRONIC ILLNESS

ANGEL HOUSE

PICKING UP THE PIECES: Musings on Chronic Illness

Published by Angel House Books
A division of Stark House Press
1315 H Street
Eureka, CA 95501, USA
griffinskye3@sbcglobal.net
www.starkhousepress.com

ISBN: 979-8-88601-060-2

Book design by Mark Shepard, shepgraphics.com

First Stark House Press/Angel House Edition: July 2024

This book began as a series of semi-monthly columns for a friend's webpage. He has graciously allowed me to publish them here for you.

Although the book is broken down into four seasons (and yes, I know they're not the ACTUAL seasons, but they make sense to me), feel free to read them in any order you choose. If you need a dash of winter in the middle of July, go for it! Can't wait for Spring? Skip ahead! Take notes, draw pictures, whatever makes this book meaningful to you.

If you or a loved one are battling a chronic illness or have become disabled, I hope you'll find understanding, compassion, and some joy sprinkled throughout these pages.

Spring

March through May

March Week 1:

You've all heard the quote by Friedrich Nietzsche, "That which does not kill us makes us stronger."

You've probably also heard the corollary, "Please. Stop. I'm strong enough."

It doesn't matter how strong you are, how weak you feel. It doesn't matter if you're having a good day or a bad week. Troubles come and go. Grief hits us all. The Bible reminds us that the rain falls on the just and the unjust alike. No one is exempt. Life is just like that. No one can be happy all the time.

For me, and maybe for you as well, it often seems that there is nothing in this world but darkness. Politics, the economy, hunger, abuse – they run rampant across our small planet. We are faced with epidemics on a daily basis as the number of deaths keeps rising. We are struggling with climate change as our weather patterns shift and bring storms we are not prepared for. We grieve with our brothers and sisters whose rights are being denied even as we struggle to understand our own privilege.

And yet, while I slept last night, the world continued to revolve on its axis. The sun is there, even if it's hidden by clouds. I have food to eat, and a warm, dry house. I have the internet to keep me connected, even if I am self-isolated. My body may not be able to do all I would ask of it, but my mind is still sharp.

You see, grief is the sword that sharpens our senses so that we can recognize joy when it arrives. You need darkness to appreciate the light. It's not always easy to remember, but the light is still shining. And the struggles of today will lead to the joys of tomorrow. Everybody struggles. It's how you choose to react to the struggles that gives you joy.

March Week 2:

They say April showers bring May flowers. Humph. I don't know about you, but I will NOT be satisfied with only flowers. I want Spring to SPRING! I want warmth, and lighter clothing and my summer jammies. It's been a long winter. Heck, it's been a long year!

But as sure as the ocean reaches the shore, Spring will come. The temperature will change, the flowers will bloom, and the renewal of nature will renew our spirits as well. We will leave the doors open and fresh breezes will blow away the cobwebs and the musty smell of old books. (Your house DOES smell like old books, right?) My husband will spend more time in the garden, pruning, planting, watering, and bringing flowers in to put on the table.

I like Spring. I like Autumn, too. I like the seasons that show us change rather than the predictability of Summer and Winter. I like variation and the unexpected. New baby birds and old crunchy leaves suit me best. Change gives me hope. Things won't always be this way. The hard times will pass and the seasons will continue to turn. Even after I've left this plane, there is comfort in knowing that the seasons will continue. The only thing that is certain is that things will change.

NOTES

March Week 3:

I am quite aware that I speak from a position of privilege. Rainy days are only fun when you are snug, safe, and warm. But that being said, in our household, we love rainy days. There's something comforting about being inside, curled up under a blanket, listening to the raindrops on the roof.

Sunny days are nice. Being able to be in the garden, or go to the beach – soaking up the Vitamin D and the warmth of the early spring sunshine – the sun feels healing to my body. But rainy days… they feel healing to my soul.

I have always loved water. From the time I could crawl into the ocean, sit on the floor of the shower, or run through the sprinkler, water has always been my element of choice. I feel at peace when I am near a large body of water – lake, river, ocean. I love boats, seagulls, the smell of the ocean, the sound of thunder, and the lapping of baby waves on my toes. Perhaps it is because I am an Aquarius. Perhaps it's because my body contains so much water. But my soul cries out for the peace that water brings.

So I watch the seagulls soar over the bay as the fishing ships bob at their moorings. I luxuriate in the hot water of my shower, feeling the spray drench my hair. And I wait for glorious, happy, snuggly rainy days.

Wonderings

March Week 4:

Revenge? Confrontation? Avoidance? Or forgiveness?

How do you handle people who have wronged you?

Recently, I have been struggling with some anger issues regarding a family member who treated me poorly. I don't like the anger. It sits, growling, somewhere near my stomach waiting to spring into action when my brain becomes too idle. I know the anger is affecting me negatively, and I want to deal with it.

The major problem for me is that the person I am angry at has died.

So, my choices are limited. Revenge and confrontation are out of the picture. Avoidance is easy, but it doesn't address my anger. That leaves forgiveness as my only option. Or does it?

I know that at some time, I will be able to forgive. I know that forgiveness is for my benefit, not theirs. I know that I will have to forgive again and again until it takes root in my soul.

But I'm not ready yet.

I've started dreaming about this person. The other night, they were in my dream, criticizing me, telling me all my choices were wrong, telling me I was too stupid to know what to do. As I struggled into wakefulness, I found myself answering them:

"You weren't always kind to me when I was alive. You criticized and treated me like I was a second-class member of the family. But I'll be damned if you can keep criticizing me now that you're dead! Not in MY house. Not in MY brain!"

…and I woke up. I felt strong, empowered, in charge of my own mind. I owned the power I have in myself and I claimed it. And I used it. And the anger lessened a little bit.

Someday, I will forgive. But for now, it is enough to recognize that they are powerless and I… I am powerful.

April Week 1:

Periodically, my husband and I like to do jigsaw puzzles. 300 piece puzzles are easy. We can shake the pieces from the box, flip them right side up, and have the puzzle completed in a couple of hours. 500 to 750 pieces take us a few days. 1000 piece puzzles can stay on the table for a week or so. We lose interest with anything larger.

We work our puzzles very differently. Hubby likes to pick up a piece and try it in many spots to see if it will fit. I like to look at the hole in the puzzle and try to find a piece to match. He likes scenic pictures, I like collages. He doesn't mind large expanses of the same color, I want constant variety. Neither of us can understand the way the other works. But together, we finish the puzzle.

There's one other aspect to puzzling that I must mention. The dining room table is against a window that has a bird feeder outside. We have swarms of finches and sparrows who come around daily to feast on the seed. We also have cats.

Now the cats know that they are not allowed on the table. But the birds are RIGHT THERE and they are sure they could reach them if we'd just get rid of the glass in the way. And sometimes, the temptation is just too much.

So when we reach a difficult part of the puzzle, when

each of us is muttering that the manufacturers must have left a piece out, one or both of us will start searching the floor. And often, we find one or more pieces that one of the cats has knocked off the table. They're not trying to mess with us, they're just being cats.

Sometimes in our lives, we are puzzled. We don't understand why things are going the way they are. We search for meaning in an incomplete picture. We want to plug the holes, but can't seem to find anything that fits. There are too many colors or not enough colors. There are too many pieces and we get bored.

But maybe we're trying to fill a hole that isn't ready to be filled. Maybe we need to work around the edges first. Maybe the pieces are upside down. Or maybe they're on the floor and we just need to pick them up. Or maybe someone DID leave a piece out of the box.

In life, as in puzzles, sometimes it's better to move on to a section that we CAN complete. And we can always come back to the missing bits. In life, as in puzzles, we can usually complete the picture eventually. And there is so much satisfaction in triumph!

April Week 2:

I have a playlist on my phone that is a mixture of all my favorite genres of music. I always hit "random" and turn up the volume whenever I'm sewing or doing chores.

This morning, I was folding the laundry when one of my favorite songs started. It's a very personal song to me. I first heard it when my then teenage son was listening to HIS music. I didn't know the name (or the band) and I just called it "that Cinderella song."

I later took it as my personal anthem when I was going through my cancer treatments. I would take my music, my crocheting, a quilt I made for my father when HE had cancer, and head for the hospital, knowing I was going to be there all day. I'd sit in the recliner and they would hook me up. The needle into my port always hurt, no matter how much numbing medicine I applied. But once it was in, the rest was pretty painless. On a physical level. The emotional toll was a lot harder. Many times I wondered whether it was worth going on.

When I turned on my music, the "Cinderella song" was always the first one I played.

It's an interesting song. It's about a girl who commits suicide and how her friend reacts to her death. Doesn't sound very uplifting, does it? Especially when you consider the position I was in. But there's a line in the chorus that hits me in the gut every time.

"Come on, try a little. Nothing is forever."

Sometimes in our lives, despair creeps in. Hope seems unattainable. Happiness is a distant memory.

Nothing is forever. Try a little.

It always lifts my spirits.

(with special thanks to The Wallflowers)

April Week 3:

I am NOT good at spontaneity. People who know me well will tell you that I start planning for Christmas in January. Birthday gifts are purchased months before the actual day. Surprises are not my best friends.

But life? Life LOVES surprises. Things going lousy? Someone will send flowers, or smile, or pay for my meal in the drive-thru. Things going well? I'm waiting for the other shoe to drop.

Many ancient sages said it, but I like the words of Thomas a Kempis best – "Man proposes, but God disposes."

For plan-makers like me, it can be difficult. But we have two choices. We can rail against fate, curse the universe, stomp our feet, and scream and cry. Or, we can take a step back. What will the latest surprise mean? Perhaps it is giving me more time to be quiet, to study my own reactions to the spontaneity of the world around me, to practice patience.

NOTES

April Week 4:

Recently, we had a death in the family. Although it was a fairly close familial relationship, I did not share a strong emotional relationship with the person. We didn't spend a lot of time together, and when we did see each other, it was all rather superficial.

And yet, I mourn. I grieve. For the life that she lived, and for the life that she lost. She was born with an illness that kept her in pain and struggling for every one of her 37 short years. She fought personal demons, societal pressures, and her own body every day of her life. And finally, her body just couldn't fight anymore. And I was glad to hear that she could finally put down the metaphorical boxing gloves and rest.

And yet… I mourn.

Why do we mourn? It's easily understandable that we grieve for loved ones we have lost. But we also grieve for strangers we never met. And we grieve for every loss in between those two extremes.

I always find comfort in John Donne's famous poem:

> "No man is an island,
> Entire of itself.
> Each is a piece of the continent,
> A part of the main.
> If a clod be washed away by the sea,

Europe is the less.
As well as if a promontory were.
As well as if a manor of thine own
Or of thine friend's were.
Each man's death diminishes me,
For I am involved in mankind.
Therefore, send not to know
For whom the bell tolls,
It tolls for thee."

And isn't that what we do? We mourn not only for those we have lost, but for ourselves. With a sense of our own mortality, we grieve that we will never see them again on this plane – that we will never know them more fully.

We grieve for those who remain – who lost someone precious to them. We grieve for those who wanted to continue living and weren't given the option.

Every loss grieves us, for the person lost is part of our own self – our "involvement in mankind." And the very fact that we can recognize that loss, and grieve for it, is a gift.

May Week 1:

Today, as I sat down to write, I found myself at a loss for words. No new ideas. No illuminating thoughts… just… blank.

I think it's because I've been going through a rough patch physically. It's hard for me to think positive or be inspired when I can't do anything more than sit on the couch and watch TV. Let's face it, Netflix doesn't exactly inspire philosophical ideas.

I miss the person I used to be. I miss dancing all night, walking in the rain, even cleaning my own house. But my life has changed. I'm not the woman I used to be. I have limitations that I could never have foreseen.

And yet, I am grateful for so many things! For the financial security of not NEEDING to work to provide for my needs. For a dry house, warm clothes, and even for Hallmark movies.

But most of all, I am thankful for my husband. He has infinite compassion towards my needs. He loves me unconditionally. And he steps in to take care of all the things I just can't manage any more.

I think that I am not the woman he married, but he thinks I am. He looks beyond the foibles and weaknesses of my body and sees straight into my heart. He cherishes me. He reminds me of the good in my life.

I know that not everyone has such a wonderful partner in their life. Some of us are alone, or with people who don't understand us. So I encourage you to cherish yourself. Look beyond the physical and mental limitations of this life and see the spiritual being you truly are.

"We are not human beings having a spiritual experience. We are spiritual beings having a human experience."
– *Pierre Teilhard de Chardin, S.J.*

May Week 2:

Do you have a junk drawer? I grew up with one drawer in the kitchen that served as a catch-all for miscellaneous things – batteries (usually dead), birthday candles, rubber bands, clothespins – anything that didn't belong somewhere else, wound up in the junk drawer. You never knew what you would find. It was a jumbled-up mess of forgotten treasures.

I still have a junk drawer, although it's pretty well organized. It still has rubber bands, clothespins, and birthday candles, but they are all separated in little drawer organizer trays. It takes a bit of the fun out of it.

But my husband and I go one better. Yes, we have a junk drawer, but we also have (dum, dum, DAAAAHHH) "The Box of Unused Cables" (trademark pending). This is shoved into a cupboard in the laundry room. Occasionally, we pull it out and sort through the cables to see if anything looks useful. There are black cables, white cables, short cables, broken cables – cables with standard three-prong plugs, some USB, and a few with weird looking ends that don't look familiar at all.

We don't need them, as everything we have obviously has a cable and is working, but you never can tell, right? So we keep them.

What do you hold on to that you don't really need? What fills the junk drawer in your kitchen? Your mind? Your heart? Are you clinging to old ideas that you know don't work or that you have replaced, just in case you need them in the future? Do you nurse old pain, keeping it alive beyond its usefulness?

Or do you hold on to happy memories? Past love? Lessons gently learned? Laughter? Kindness?

Fill your junk drawer with useful things. Clean out the old, broken, and useless. Organize the helpful and useful and separate them so you can find them easily. Or leave them all tumbled together in your mind and heart so that, when you reach in, you get a happy surprise!

May Week 3:

A broken bone. A broken tooth. A broken heart.

A break in the skin. A mental break down. A broken spirit.

Humans are fragile. We break so easily. Fortunately, most breaks can be mended thanks to modern medicine. We get a cast, or stitches, or a root canal, and the broken bits slowly heal.

The internal breaks are more difficult. The ones that don't show. Some of them never heal. The loss of a loved one. The shattered dream. The lost faith.

Perhaps you have heard of the Japanese art of kintsukuroi or kintsugi (　). When a treasured piece of pottery gets broken, the artist repairs the break with a lacquer mixed with gold, silver, or platinum. The resulting piece is different than the original, but just as beautiful. As a philosophy, Kintsugi treats breaks and repairs as part of the whole of the object. They are not something to disguise, but something to be embraced – to be accepted as they are.

Sometimes, it seems that we focus wholly on our flaws, our scars and broken bits. We each strive to mend and to cover and to hide what we see as our imperfections. We try to fill the broken bits with food, or sex, or busy-ness. We are ashamed.

I have come to a period of my life where I am

becoming more accepting of myself. More comfortable with my flaws. More understanding of my imperfections. Oh, I have a lot of them, but I earned every one through the experiences of my life. They make me who I am. And I am going to try to fill the holes with the precious metals of life – laughter, happy memories, and love.

"There is a crack in everything, that's how the light gets in."   – *Leonard Cohen*

May Week 4:

Goals are fantastic things. Determination to achieve a specified outcome can change your life. Every business I have ever worked for has, at some point, asked me for a five-year plan, or a ten-year plan.

"Where do you see yourself in five years?" Oh, how I dread hearing that.

Creating a goal, setting a plan to achieve that goal, striving to meet it. These are truly admirable ideas. But… life has a way of changing or interrupting goals. Jobs change, family dynamics shift, health and strength wax and wane. Sometimes, through no fault of our own, goals cannot be reached. Does that mean that we failed?

Instead of goals, I like to have hopes to go with my plans. I hope to achieve the end result. I hope that my life path leads me to a desired ending. I can plan, and work, and push to achieve the outcome, but I can also accept that I do not have total control over what happens. I can rest when I need to. I can change my goals and plans. I can adapt. That's one of the best things about being human. We are adaptable.

So make your goals. Set them high. Shoot for the stars! Just remember that when change happens (and it WILL happen) to be flexible – to adapt and accept. And always hope for the best possible outcome.

THOUGHTS

Extra Spring thoughts:

Sometimes, I feel overwhelmed. I think it's genetic, or at least passed down the distaff side of our family. My aunt used to say, "We are female. We are Browns. It must be our fault."

"It," of course, applies to anything in life. War, gas prices, illnesses, hunger… you name it, we take on the responsibility.

Add to that the fact that I am an empath. Any one person's troubles feel like my own troubles. I know rationally that they are NOT my problems, but they feel like it.

So I get overwhelmed. And I get overwhelmed by happy things, too! I have 100 movies on my Netflix list. I have more yarn and fabric than any one person could use in their lifetime. My "to be read" pile is so high I can't find the bottom. And I grieve for the movies I will never get to see, the books I will never get to read, the fabric and yarn that will still be there after I die. It's overwhelming.

One night recently, I was so overwhelmed that I was just about in tears. I was lying in bed with my husband and telling him how awful it was. There's illness, hungry children, bombs, gun violence… the list goes on. And I was telling him how awful I felt because I just couldn't fix it all.

And then it dawned on me. No one is asking me to fix the entire world. NO ONE IS ASKING ME!!

I am not responsible for the world. I cannot fix world hunger, or mass shootings, or the ignorance and insensitivity I see. I heard someone say the other day that all you can do is try to be a little bit better person today than you were yesterday. And if we could all do that for ourselves, for our little corner… the world would take care of itself.

Ruminations

SUMMER

June through August

June Week 1:

Christmas is coming.

I know several of you are probably throwing your hands up in the air, aghast at the thought of the holidays. Why would you want to wish the year away?

But I can feel it. Christmas is coming.

Those of you who are crafters know of what I speak. It is time to get supplies, to plan the schedule, to decide who will get a home-made gift this year. It's not too soon to start that painting or knitting or poetry. Christmas is coming!

But what about today???

I envy my dog, my cats, and my husband. They are much better at living in the moment than I am. And too often, I lose the moment in worrying about the past or planning for the future.

It's a balance. Making plans, starting projects, planting a tree – they all remind us that we will have a future to look forward to. But sitting in the moment, enjoying what IS, just for today, makes the present worth living.

So I hope that you are making plans. But I hope you're doing it at the beach, or in a deck chair, or lying in a hammock, or cozied up on your favorite chair. I hope you find the balance between memories of the past, the essence of the present, and the hopes for the future.

After all, even Scrooge finally came to see that he needed the spirits of all the Christmases – past, present, and future. They all have lessons to teach.

June Week 2:

Anyone who has ever had to write for a deadline – student, author, journalist – will tell you that it's hard. You sit, staring at your notebook, your typewriter, your laptop, waiting for inspiration. You try to spark a thought by washing the dishes, watching TV, playing with your cat. You delay and push away and ignore. But eventually, you write. Sometimes it's not worth reading. Sometimes, it's genius. Often, it's cathartic.

I usually write about what's going on in my life. Recently, I wrote about a deceased relative. I was still angry with them and having problems dealing with the anger. But writing it down, putting it out there into the universe, has changed me. I have come to a better understanding.

I have found forgiveness.

Forgiveness doesn't mean that they didn't hurt me. It doesn't mean that the treatment I received was fair or deserved. It means that I can let go of the anger and move on with my life. It means that the power within me is great enough to allow them THEIR hurts, THEIR anger, without letting it dictate how I will lead my life. It means that I can accept that the past is in the past. I can't change it, but I can learn from it.

Anger runs deep in my family, and I have passed it on to others far too often. But the older I grow, the quicker I am to apologize, to seek forgiveness for my own actions. I am trying to break the intergenerational pattern.

I have learned that breaking a pattern consists of three parts:

First, seeing the behavior after the fact. Looking back and seeing how your behavior affected you and others.

Secondly, seeing the behavior as it happens. Recognizing that your actions in the NOW are not representing who you want to be.

Thirdly, recognizing the behavior BEFORE it happens. It might only be a second before it happens, or it might be a week – it depends on the pattern you are trying to change. But once you can anticipate the behavior, you can make a different choice. You can choose a DIFFERENT behavior.

That's when the pattern shatters into pieces – when you realize you are free to make a different choice. That's when you can forgive.

June Week 3:

When my laundry baskets get full, my husband swoops in and delivers them to the washing machine for me. Later, he brings it back to me, all warm and snuggly from the dryer, and tells me it is done. And then I leave it in the basket for anywhere from 2 days to several weeks, burrowing to find the item I need and steadfastly ignoring the rest of it. Sometimes, it never does make it to the closet or drawers, but simply piles up until he washes it again.

I don't like folding laundry.

HOWEVER… Summertime laundry is so much easier to deal with than wintertime. Everything is lighter, smaller, easier to fold. More fits in the basket so hubby doesn't have to do as many loads. And I am more likely to fold and put it away when it only takes a few minutes. Winter laundry seems to take hours to put away. Flannel nightgowns, sweatshirts, sweatpants, heavy sweaters, socks… it just goes on and on. It covers the entire bed even when it's folded! Summer laundry takes 10 minutes, tops. Four small piles of t-shirts, shorts, jammies, and underwear. Folded neatly and tucked into the drawers and I can move on with my day, feeling virtuous and organized.

I don't mind admitting that I feel a bit proud of having done such a minor chore. But I think the best part of it is knowing that I made things a bit easier for my husband. The baskets are empty, and I can put dirty items back in them instead of just letting them pile up somewhere. He won't have to go hunting when it's time to do laundry again. It ain't much, but it's honest work.

June Week 4:

I was raised to respect the flag. We said the Pledge of Allegiance every day in school. I believed in the freedoms of my country and the dream of liberty and justice for all.

It hasn't turned out that way. We, as a country, have not lived up to the dream. We have given power to a small, select group while demeaning and deposing those who didn't fit the mold. We have stood by through genocide, incarceration, murder, slavery, and police brutality. We have built concentration camps, prisons, glass ceilings, and border walls.

Sometimes, I am not proud to be an American.

Yet the dream persists. From Abraham Lincoln to Martin Luther King, the United States has always held up the dream of a better way of life, a better country, a better world.

When I was in college, I read a book discussing contemporary issues and the morality affecting them. It suggested that you should always look at the issues and decide… were they moving towards freedom? Toward justice? Towards equality?

Politics is a pendulum. It swings from side to side, left to right, with not much time in the middle. But isn't the middle where we want to be? Don't we want an even playing field for everyone? Don't we want to rest at the center, knowing that all of the people in our country are also at rest?

I consider myself a patriot. I believe in the dream of our country. I don't think we're there yet, but I believe we can get there.

July Week 1:

Independence is prized in the United States. We even celebrate the day that the United States became independent of British rule. But are we truly independent?

As a country, we are dependent upon other countries for the products we import such as oil, machinery (including computers), pharmaceuticals, and plastics. We could create much of what we import here in our own country, but it isn't cost effective. We barter a bit of freedom for lower prices.

As a city, town, or county, we are dependent upon the state (which is, in turn, dependent upon the federal government) for roads, schools, and other infrastructure. And we are dependent upon other counties, cities, states, and countries for food and products that are not available locally.

As a community of family and friends, we are dependent on each other for comfort, care, and companionship, for teaching and learning, and for love and acceptance.

Independence is often used as a synonym for freedom. Freedom from persecution, freedom of religion, freedom of speech. Every person has freedom in their thoughts and feelings and every person is free to reap the consequences of their actions and their speech.

So celebrate the little every day freedoms that surround you. Freedom to love, to laugh, to dream. And spare a thought for those who have lost their freedoms, those in prisons not of their own making, whether they be physical, mental, social, or spiritual. And above all, recognize that we, as humans, are gloriously dependent upon each other.

July Week 2:

My brain lies to me.

I read recently that not everyone has voices in their head. That astounds me! I have so many voices that I can't always tell them apart! My parents, my husband, previous therapists and ministers, teachers, children… they all have something to say on any given day. Sometimes they're helpful; sometimes, not so much.

Then there are those other voices. I refer to them as the "yaddas." You know, "Yadda do this. Yadda do that. Yadda clean the house. Yadda read a book." They seem to be the most loquacious, always chiming in when there's an empty space. They, like nature, abhor a vacuum. And they are hardly ever helpful.

But the worst voice, the one that whispers to me late at night? That's the voice that lies. That voice tells me that I am a burden. It says that I am worthless. It wants me to believe that I am alone and that no one ever did or ever will love me the way that I am. It gets louder when I am tired. It suggests that I am sicker than I really am. It urges me to cry and sneers when I am denied the release of tears.

I don't know where that voice came from. It seems that it has always been there. It's the voice that kicks me when I'm down.

But it lies. And therein I find my strength. It's taken me a long time, but I no longer believe what that voice tells me. It is wrong. It doesn't know who I truly am. It lies. And by remembering that, the voice can be banished – at least temporarily.

I remember that I am "fearfully and wonderfully made." I know that I have a purpose on this earth. I delight in those who have given me love and support throughout my life. I can own my weaknesses and rely on my strengths. I can recite a litany of the good things about myself. And that power, that self-knowledge, allows me to claim my truth and prove the voice a liar.

July Week 3:

"I'm late! I'm late!
  For a very important date!
  No time to say, 'Hello'. 'GOODBYE!'
  I'm late! I'm late! I'm late!"

Bob Hilliard

A therapist once told me that if you're early, you're paranoid. If you're on time, you're compulsive. And if you're late, you're hostile.

I am ALWAYS on time. Or early. I hate being late to things. I think that I must have been taught that it's rude to show up late to things. Or maybe it's a side effect of my anxiety. I don't even like to cut it close. I'd rather park outside an event for 15 minutes waiting for the right time to go in than risk being a couple of minutes late.

But then there's the brain fog… it taunts me, torments me. My husband and I both live off the idea that if it's not on the calendar, it doesn't exist. We just don't remember things like we used to. So sometimes, I *am* late. Or miss things entirely.

And you know what? That's OK. My being late doesn't mean the world stops turning. I don't have to run myself down or whine and complain. I can just apologize and move on. I can accept my humanity and my mistakes. I can relax a little.

PONDERINGS

July Week 4:

Sometimes, if it's a good day and I feel like I have a bit of energy, I like to go for a walk. It's especially tempting when the sun is out and the flowers are blooming in our garden.

I never go very far… around the block is about my limit. On a REALLY good day, I might even try TWO blocks! But if I overestimate my capabilities, I may find myself sitting on the seat of my walker at a distance from home base. Of course, if I'm really done in, I could call my husband, and he would come get me. But I try to finish my walk if I possibly can.

So I sit there, panting, and I ponder. How should I get back home? Is it shorter to go back the way I came? Or to keep going? How long should I rest? Is anyone headed in my direction that looks like a threat?

Everyone faces their own challenges. For some of us, it's physical. For others, emotional, spiritual, or mental. Everyone faces their own difficult journey at times. Winston Churchill once said, "If you're going through hell, keep going." But… is it shorter to go back? Is it easier? Faster? Obviously, if you need to go back to save yourself, that's what you do. But what if you're halfway through? What if you're only half a block from your house?

You keep going. You've already viewed the scenery

behind you. You know what the past looks like. Why not forge ahead and see something different? You may need to rest, but you will get safely home, just the same.

August Week 1:

"Resilience is accepting your new reality, even if it's less good than the one you had before. You can fight it, you can do nothing but scream about what you've lost, or you can accept that and try to put together something that's good."

Elizabeth Edwards

Oh, how I struggle with this! It's in my nature to see the loss. Just when I think I've accepted the changes in my life, something else will crop up and make me notice them again. I try not to whine or fuss, but my husband will tell you that sometimes I just HAVE to whine. It's not fair.

When I was growing up, my mother used to say "Well, Cindy, life isn't always fair." But she was wrong. Life IS always fair. Everyone gets sunshine. Everyone gets rain. No one gets to choose when the good times come or when the bad times seem overwhelming. Common experiences connect us, even the bad ones.

And you know, it's okay to whine about your problems sometimes! It reminds others that we all share the difficult times and it gives them the opportunity to help us. But, as I try to remember, it's not good to complain too often. It leaves your focus on the negative. And it can negatively affect your listeners. They have troubles, too. It's important to make opportunities for everyone to talk, and for everyone to listen. And maybe, just maybe, you can help them with their problems.

And being able to help a loved one is a very big positive. And love is never lost.

August Week 2:

Three easy steps to have a productive day:

Get a good night's sleep. Not always easy for us insomniacs. Sometimes I follow all the rules, and I still can't sleep. I meditate, count my blessings, regulate my breathing… nothing. If thoughts are running around in my head, making a list sometimes helps. I get up, write down all the to-dos that are running races inside my head, and then I can forget about them. But sometimes, my brain goes on down the memory rabbit hole and it insists on parading every error, every misstep, every embarrassment. Around and around… And everyone knows that the more you need a good night's sleep, the less likely you will get one. So I read, or get up, or sleep in another room. It doesn't give me a good night's sleep, but at least I get *some* sleep.

Start the day with a plan. What am I going to accomplish? I usually have a list a mile long. I know I can't do all of it, but at least it's a place to start. Of course, I didn't get much sleep (see item number 1), so I only have so much energy. What is on my list that I can handle today? I ought to do some housework, but I know I don't have the oomph for that. Is my brain sharp? Can I work on the computer? Write, pay bills, that kind of thing? Or maybe I am up to sitting at the sewing machine. I can sew something. Oh, but first I have to cut something out. I don't think I can handle that, so sewing is out. TV. I can always manage TV. And I can usually crochet. That's my fall back. But how many scarves can one person use? Sigh. Apparently, one more.

Eat properly. Vegetables, protein, fruit, low carbs, whole grains. Eating well boosts your mood and clears your thinking. But cooking takes energy, and peanut butter on toast is easy. Take-out is easy, too. And canned chili is always good. Oops. I missed this rule, too. Oh, look! It's 7:30. I can justifiably (in my own mind) go to bed. I was productive. Kind of. I got up, got dressed, and made it to the couch. Some days, that's plenty to be proud of.

August Week 3:

There's a fine line between persistence and stubbornness. Sometimes, I cross that line. Recently, we were doing some major cleaning and organizing. I looked at a large box filled with magazines and said to myself, "You can do this! You can move that box!" This is where the stubbornness kicked in. Now I know I have a less than sturdy back. But by gum! I was going to move that box! And I did. I not only moved it, I picked it up and put it on top of another box. I did everything right. I bent my knees, used my legs, and moved slowly. I felt great – strong, capable, empowered – until about noon the next day when I suddenly couldn't stand or bend without sending my lower back into spasms.

Getting older ain't for sissies, and it usually comes with a few aches and pains. This was not my first go around with sciatica, so I had my husband break out the heating pad and the Tylenol and resigned myself to spending several days on the couch. Me spending time on the couch is a lot like being quarantined. It's not that different from my usual daily routine, but I resent it anyway. It takes away my OPTION to sit on the couch, my OPTION to go outside, my OPTION to participate in hobbies.

Soon, I will be able to go to the grocery store. Family is coming to visit. I will be back to "normal." And I KNOW, that within a couple of weeks, I will be wanting to spend a day sitting on the couch. I will crave the solitude and quiet that being in my own space brings. I will long for the alone-ness. And the only difference will be the options that I have.

Sometimes, options are taken away from us. Sometimes we have so many options we find it difficult to choose. But when we have options, we must choose carefully. We must choose to be kind, to others and to ourselves. We must be grateful for the options and cheerfully release those we don't choose. Because every option, even those we don't choose, change us and form us into our future selves.

> "Two roads diverged in a wood, and I–
>   I took the one less traveled by,
>   And that has made all the difference."
>
> – *Robert Frost*

August Week 4:

As a child, my favorite amusement park ride was the carousel. I would race to get my favorite horse, often with my father by my side. He would scoop me up to place me in the saddle, and he would stay right beside me to make sure I didn't fall.

Truth be told, I still love to ride the carousel. I don't race the children for the best horse, but I do make sure I have one that goes up and down. The stationary animals don't do it for me.

Yesterday was a good day. I had energy, my back felt fine, and I was happy. I pulled out a huge pile of fabric to cut out some new projects. Throughout the day, I cut 3 pairs of knickers, a pair of pants, and 4 shirts for my husband. When all that was done, I went into the sewing room and magically converted it from total chaos to merely untidy. I was so excited and pleased! I made plans. I was going to get up today and sew like crazy!

Today, I'm on the couch with my pain meds and heating pad. My back is screaming and won't let me do anything else.

My life is a merry-go-round.

Sometimes, life is up. Happiness and high energy days can make me nearly giddy. When I feel good physically, I feel good mentally. But sometimes, life is down. I can hurt, or be sad, or feel frustrated at my physical limitations. I get grumpy.

But whatever kind of day I'm having, up or down, happy or sad, the merry-go-round keeps turning. And another day will come. And it may be up. Or down. There's no telling in advance (of, if only!). But it will be different than today, that's for sure.

Some people say that a merry-go-round is useless. You go up and down and around and around, but never truly get anywhere. But I try to remember to focus on the ride. To remember the joy of childhood and the security of my father making sure I didn't fall.

I never did fall off my horse. And I was always ready to go again.

Extra Summer Thoughts:

My mother was an artist. In her younger days, she painted with oils, my favorite piece being a still life in reds and golds. She set aside her art to raise us kids, but in later years she took it up again. She switched to watercolors and started painting abstracts. Her colors swirled across the paper, evoking leaves, or wind, or rocks.

I envied her talent.

Sometimes, I'll be surfing the internet and run across a musician whose work is so breathtakingly lovely that I stand in awe of what they can accomplish. Their fingers dance over piano keys or guitar strings, or their voices find notes I never knew existed, soaring into the heavens.

I envy their talent.

As I read, late at night in the silence of my bedroom, I will sometimes run across a phrase that makes me laugh, or tugs at my heart, or crystallizes an idea that I have always thought but couldn't express. I marvel at the author's ability to create this tiny jewel of typewritten prose.

I envy their talent.

It's not that I don't have skills of my own. I sew, crochet, knit, paint a little, write a little… But that's just it. I think of these things as skills, not talent. I think that anyone could do what I do. It's not that difficult.

But maybe I'm wrong. Maybe the singing or the painting or the writing that others amaze me with is easy for them. Maybe they think that anyone could do what they do. And maybe, just maybe, they wish they could sew.

I don't want to be a famous artist or musician or author. I am content to sew a little, knit a little, write a little. My talents suit me. They are deeply ingrained and very personal.

I bet yours suit you, too.

Contemplations

AUTUMN

SEPTEMBER
THROUGH
NOVEMBER

CYNTHIA L. SHEPARD

September Week 1:

To me, September has always been the beginning of Autumn. I'm old enough that the first day of school was always the day after the Labor Day weekend. September meant new clothes, new books and teachers, colder nights, colorful trees.

September is about change. It's a chance to start fresh. Preconceived notions about who I am, who I should be, what I can do can be tossed away and I can start again.

My husband and I like to travel in September. The crowds have died down and the weather is still nice. We were married in September (Happy Anniversary, Honey!) so we often go away to celebrate.

Travel isn't as easy as it used to be. Remember getting in the car and just seeing how far you can drive in a day? Yeah. Not going to happen anymore. But I am very good at planning and organizing. I've learned a lot of tricks along the way. I make lists and reservations. We make a file folder with maps, receipts, and tickets. I plan and start packing a week in advance while my husband waits till the last minute and throws things into a bag.

Travel, to me, is about change. I get to see new things, meet new people, try new adventures. Controlled chaos – plan, but be ready (and open) for anything.

Change can be scary, but change is good. Without change, we would stagnate and die. As you move into September, I hope you open your arms and race headlong into the new season of change with joy (and a maybe a bit of trepidation) in your heart.

September Week 2:

We are all human. We are all alike. And yet, we are all different. Every body has its own genetic makeup, its own peculiarities. I have green eyes; my husband's eyes are blue. My family is tall; yours may be short.

One of my body's unique properties relates to sleep. For me to feel at my best, happy, productive, I need about 10 hours of solid sleep. If only it were that easy. Some nights, I get 6 hours. Some nights (most nights) I get about 8 hours. But a few times a month, I will get 10 or 11 hours of sleep. It's a funny combination of being just the right temperature, having just the right covers, the right amount of fresh air, the right seal on my CPAP mask, the right blood sugar, and the right meds. When all of those things align (probably with the stars and planets), I sleep.

And oh, what a difference to the day ahead! I wake up cheerful. I have a little bit more energy. My brain is clearer. I feel that I can move mountains! (I settle for folding the laundry or doing a little sewing.) I am kinder, more forgiving, more patient. I like myself more.

So every night I try to duplicate the magic formula. Sometimes it works, most times it doesn't. But I recognize the difference. I know how sleep changes me.

What makes you more kind, more productive,

happier? Is it sleep? Diet? Meditation or prayer? Or some combination of all these things. Maybe you don't know? I encourage you to look at patterns in your life and try to understand those things that improve your days. Whatever it is that makes a difference for you, I hope you pursue it. Recognize it, give it a priority in your life. And rejoice when it all comes together.

September Week 3:

"School Days, School Days,
  Dear Old Golden Rule Days…"
                              – Cobb and Edwards

I always had a love/hate relationship with school. On the one hand, I love learning. I love sitting in a classroom, taking notes, hearing new ideas and theories. On the other hand, I am not a social butterfly by any stretch of the imagination. I never had many friends and I never seemed to fit in. And my love of learning didn't make me popular.

Public school is about fitting into the norm. Kids can be mean. Anyone who is different is singled out – whether they are too smart, too plain, too quiet, too loud… they are perceived as different and not "normal."

And yet…

What IS normal? I use to have a shirt that said "Jesus wasn't normal." The best and brightest among us aren't normal. They are exceptional. While we think of the word "exceptional" as meaning "above average," it also means not typical – not normal.

I firmly believe that, as human beings, we are more alike than we are different. But it's the differences that seem to get all the attention. In the divisive political atmosphere of the day, differences are constantly being called out, denigrated, made fun of, and ostracized. But, really, whether you're LGBTQ+ or straight, able bodied or handicapped, Muslim, Jewish, Christian, or atheist, black, white, or any color in between, are we not all the same?

Do we not all want what's best for ourselves and our children? Do we not all love, grieve, fear? Do we not all hope for peace and happiness?

Are we not all truly the same where it counts?

September Week 4:

I have very vivid dreams. There's lots of action and colors and people. Recently, I found myself in a work situation that was very frustrating and it showed up in my dreams.

In my dream, all I had to do was get from one place to another, but the way was filled with traps and puzzles and people who wanted to talk to me. It was like a bad reality game show with a bit of Indiana Jones tossed in. And I kept getting pushed back to the start. At one point, I lost my footing and was hit in the back by a very large plank. At another point, I found myself in mid-air with a parachute and a bunch of other people and we were falling. Below us I could see all the other teams that had tried and failed.

I never did get to where I was going, but I finally woke up. And my first thought was, "Well, at least I persevered."

As a child, I was told I was stubborn. As an adult, I was told that I could accomplish whatever I set my mind to. It's an interesting comparison.

The flip side of stubbornness is persistence. We all go through frustrating times, difficult times, horrifying times. And yet, here we are, still kicking. We persevere and, hopefully, find a way through to the finish.

Brainwaves!

October Week 1:

On paper I am sooooo organized. Travel plans, finances, Christmas cards, to do lists… I have a spreadsheet for everything!

In practice… well, not so much.

About a year ago, I ordered some silicon finger sleeves so that I could use my hot glue gun without burning my fingers. In due time, they arrived and, true to my nature, I set them aside. At some point, I was tidying up, found them, and "put them away."

Now a truly organized person would put them away with the glue gun. I mean, that's only logical, don't you think? Yeah, not so much.

Several times during the past year, I have looked for those finger sleeves. I mean, they have to be SOMEWHERE in the craft room, right? And now, with projects a-plenty, I find I am using my glue gun more frequently. But my fingers must continue to suffer as the protection I purchased is nowhere to be found.

A few days ago, I went into my sewing/craft room to finish some pillows for sale. I have been in there every day lately as I finished up the goodies for the sale. This day, I found a plastic bag sitting in the middle of the room. It hadn't been there on the day before, but today it was smack in the middle of the room. I grabbed it to throw it away, but it had weight to it. Something was in there.

BEHOLD! My finger protectors!

I reorganized that whole room this summer and there was no bag. Where had they been all year? How did the bag appear in the middle of the floor? Why now, when I needed it most?

In my house, we call that a Christmas Miracle. Whether you credit the universe, fortuosity, or just plain luck, I am grateful. (And yes, this time I put them WITH the hot glue gun.)

October Week 2:

I use Facebook quite a bit. It keeps me in touch with friends and family around the world. One of the things that I like the most are the memories. Every day, Facebook shows me what I was doing 1 year ago, or 5 years ago, or 15 years ago. There are so many happy memories! And some awful ones as well.

Sometimes it's hard to tell the difference between a happy memory and a sad one. If I can remember how I felt on any given day, those happy memories are fantastic! But if I compare them to the life I live now, they make me sad.

In 2010, I took the train to Santa Fe, New Mexico. I went by myself and I walked all over that town. It was beautiful! The pictures I took are incredible to see. I had such a wonderful time!

In 2018, hubby and I went to London. I walked all over that town, too, but it damn near killed me. On our last day, I collapsed outside the train station with muscle spasms in my back, sobbing, exhausted, and knowing I had to get to the station or I couldn't get back to our hotel.

Today, my husband and I talk about travelling and one of the big concerns is how I will get around. I HATE that I cannot just get up and go anymore. I want to create more happy memories, but I often feel imprisoned by this body that contains the real me.

Picking up the pieces means accepting my limitations. It means that I can't travel if travel requires a lot of walking. It means I can't set up a tent anymore, so camping is out of the question. It means that I have to depend on my husband and other people to help me. It's hard.

And yet, I have had so many wonderful travel experiences in my life – more than many people ever have the opportunity to try. And I am so very grateful!

If this is resonating with you, if you are chafing at the limitations of your physical being, your finances, your skills, I hope that you have happy memories to carry you through. I hope that you can remember times when you rose above your limitations, when you did more than you thought possible, and when your heart was filled to bursting with joy!

October Week 3:

I am grateful (OK, I force myself to be grateful) for so many things. In the midst of despair, I force myself to count my blessings. It's not the big things that matter (although those are important, too), but the little things that make me grateful. In fact, as I think about it, maybe the little things ARE the big things!

Electricity – I wouldn't get through a summer, even in Eureka, without my electric fan. And in the winter, my electric blanket.

Clean running water – there are so many people around the world (many in our own country) who do not have clean drinking water. I am so blessed to have it at the turn of a tap.

Food – I never have to worry about my next meal.

Clean clothes – I have an abundance of things to wear for any occasion. Of course, I usually default to sweats or pajamas, but I have options! And I have a washer and dryer and husband to keep them clean.

Voting – the politicians may not always do what I want, but at least I have some small say in who's in charge.

Pets – Currently, we have a small flock of birds, 2 cats, and a small, barky dog. There is always someone to entertain me (or annoy me) and I always have companionship.

Home – home is a combination of all the little things. Pets, food, comfort, water, power, my husband, my couch… all the things that make my life worth living are right here, in my home.

I am grateful. And gratitude improves an attitude.

It doesn't mean it is easy, or that we don't suffer in the process, but we do it. We climb the mountains, ford the streams, slash our way through the underbrush, and struggle through.

Maybe we won't wind up where we thought we would. Maybe the end result won't be worth the effort we put into it. But doesn't the struggle have value in itself? And who knows, maybe the end result will be better than we ever dreamed!

October Week 4:

"From *ghoulies* and *ghosties*
  And long-leggedy beasties
  And things that go bump in the night,
  Good Lord, deliver us!"
      – *(old Scottish prayer)*

I am Scottish by heritage. And the women in my family have always had a touch of the "sight." We know when loved ones need us, however far away they may be. My mother did past-life regression. I read the Tarot. We believe in ghosts. We've just always dabbled a bit in the other-worldly. It seems normal to me, but I know some other people find it a bit scary.

Some people love to play at the edge of danger, while others prefer to stay home, safe and sound. Roller coasters, skydiving, spelunking… they are all a bit scary (maybe a lot scary) and certainly not crucial to our well-being, so why do we choose to be scared?

I think it's because we know how frightening life can be. The world is a big, scary place with horrors and traumas waiting around every corner. Just read the news and you can be overwhelmed by the terrors in the world.

So we choose smaller, manageable terrors — things

that we can be fairly comfortable with – to prove to ourselves that we can handle the fear. We learn how to handle our emotions and our reactions by playing at being afraid. It helps us to handle the big fears when we know we can handle the small fears. It reminds us that we are brave.

November Week 1:

Nov 1

"And when October goes
  The snow begins to fly
  Above the smokey roofs
  I watch the planes go by.
  The children running home
  Beneath a twilight sky,
  Oh, for the fun of them
  When I was one of them…"
  – *Barry Manilow/Johnny Mercer*

I can't ignore it any longer. Summer is gone. I tried to hold onto it as long as I could, but it's time. The days grow shorter, the nights grow colder, and it's time.

I huddle beneath blankets as I watch TV and drink hot cocoa. I unpack the flannel jammies that I hid away last April. I feel the cold ache in my bones.

Perhaps it's just that, as I grow older, the years go zipping by faster than ever. Each year is a fraction of my life. When I was four, a year was a quarter of my life, so it seemed to last forever. Now, each year is a sliver of the time I have spent on this planet and the sliver gets smaller all the time.

October has gone, and winter is creeping in.

Wonderings

November Week 2:

Perseverance. Determination. Drive. Stamina. Tenacity.

What comes to mind when you think of perseverance? I bet you think of running a race, or completing a task, or soldiering on against all odds. But why? Why do we glorify "toughing it out" instead of celebrating "giving up?" "Giving up" has such a negative connotation. But sometimes, giving up is the best thing we can do. Sometimes, we are running races that we just can't win. And maybe we shouldn't win those races!

Maybe it's not really our race to run. Maybe we're trying to do someone else's job. Maybe what we are sacrificing to persist in our path is worth more than we are gaining. Maybe we are causing more damage than we know.

I challenge you to consider… maybe our existence is enough.

Maybe it is enough that we take deep breaths, enjoy the beauty around us, love our neighbors, cultivate peace and joy.

So I invite you to "give up." Give up the tasks that cause you pain – physical, mental, spiritual. Give up the unfinished projects that bring you guilt instead of pleasure. Give up running races that require help from others who are NOT willing to run beside you.

It's OK to "give up." It's OK to know your own limits. You do not have to complete every race. It is more than enough to simply exist.

November Week 3:

I am married to a wonderful man who likes taking care of me. He cooks, cleans, does the errands... and I usually feel guilty that, because of my various illnesses, I can't do more for him.

Today I had an epiphany — an AHA moment.

When I was a child, it was instilled into me at a very young age that it was my job to take care of others. I tried, even as a child, to make things right for my family. As I grew into adulthood, I was the one you could depend on. My mom once said that if you wanted something done, you just asked me. That one way or another I would figure out how to do whatever it was.

When I got married the first time, I tried everything I knew to do to become the woman my husband wanted, often at the sacrifice of my own mental or physical health.

In my second marriage, I did the same, bending over backwards to ensure that my husband would be happy and comfortable. Right up until the day I told him I wanted a divorce.

Today, my wonderful (third) husband and I were discussing growing older and dying. I told him I felt that I needed to be useful or there was no point in wanting to stay alive – that life itself was not enough.

After we came into the house, I realized. AHA! All of my life I struggled to give, to care for, to help, to provide, to be useful. Maybe now, it's my time to learn how to be helped, provided for, and how to receive graciously.

Maybe that's the lesson to be gained in being physically limited. Maybe it's time I learned how to be loved.

November Week 4:

If you have ever wanted a lesson in perseverance, adopt a cat or two and a very furry dog. How does this teach perseverance?

Fleas.

Fleas are one of the most difficult pests to get rid of. You have to de-flea each animal. You have to sprinkle flea powder in all your furniture. You must vacuum the flea powder up because yes, they live inside your vacuum bag. You must wash all bedding, theirs and yours.

And you have to do all of this for at least three weeks to end the life cycle of the fleas that have made it into your house.

Go ahead. Ask me how I know.

But in the end, our house will be cleaner and our much-loved critters will be healthier. And we will have, hopefully, learned a lesson. Keeping ahead of the issue is so much easier than rectifying the problem. And isn't that true with most things. If we take our meds, get some gentle exercise, meditate, BEFORE we encounter a crisis, it's much easier to make it through in one piece.

NOTES

Extra Autumn Thoughts:

What is truth? It is difficult to nail down these days as more and more "truths" seem mutable or subjective to one's own experience.

Are facts true? I mean, I think we can all agree that in our current numbering system, 2+2=4, but I'm sure there are those on the internet who would dispute that as false. The sky appears blue on a sunny day. Is that true? It depends upon your vision, or location, or understanding of the word "blue." And after all, the sky is really every color except blue. Blue is the color it reflects back to our eyes – it's the color of light that the sky it refuses to absorb. So, while it may be true that one or more of us perceive the sky to be blue, it is really composed of every other color of light. It rejects being "blue."

What is the truth of who you are? Are you everything you absorb, while only letting others see what you reject? I know, for myself, my internal truth changes with my emotions, my age, and my health. On any given day I may see myself as grumpy, or kind, or troublesome, or sad. And if the idea I have of myself is that changeable, is it really true?

Of course, humans are more than just the things we absorb. We are extremely complicated. And without getting into the whole nature vs. nurture debate, I would posit that the truth about any one of us is that we are made up of some of both – the soul we are born with and the experiences we have along the way. Plus, of course, some star dust and a couple of dust bunnies for texture.

So take a look at who you are. Be true to yourself. And be gentle with yourself. You are the only you in the whole world! And no one does it better.

THOUGHTS

96

December through February

CYNTHIA L. SHEPARD

December Week 1:

Imagine yourself in a cozy cabin, deep in the woods. The fireplace crackles as it sheds a glow over the wood-paneled room. A table is set with crockery and linens. You relax in a cane-back chair while all your loved ones sit around the table. Conversation is effortless

– friendly and warm. Laughter dominates as stories – old and new – are shared.

Now, with your permission, let's invite my grandmother – a stocky, stolid woman with snow white hair and a seldom seen smile. She putters back and forth between the table and the stove, ladling out chicken and home-made noodles and serving fresh baked lemon meringue pie. Suddenly, she stops and speaks, "Listen."

Everyone quiets and turns to hear as she continues, "Listen. It's snowing."

There is a certain type of silence that snow brings. It muffles even the little sounds of birds and forest creatures. It damps down the everyday and creates a sacred silence.

A few weeks ago, I was having trouble sleeping. I put on a guided imagery meditation to see if it would help. It focused on silence. First, you must listen to all the sounds – trucks, sirens, your pets, the refrigerator

– all of the sounds you can hear. Then, and only then, can you hear the silence. It's there. It's BETWEEN the sounds, between your own breaths, between your heartbeats. Silence.

Then, you realize how your thoughts go running through your head – worries, things to do, memories – and you notice that, once again, there is silence. It's BETWEEN the thoughts, between the neurons firing. Silence.

Accept the silence. Honor the silence. Rest in the silence. Live in the silence.

Peace is in the silence.

December Week 2:

Growing up, Christmas was my favorite holiday. I mean, cookies, presents, candy, Santa – what's not to like? But what was always most important to me, what truly made the holiday special, was the tree. I would lay on the floor, peering up through the branches as the twinkling lights reflected in the glass ornaments. I would breathe deeply the scent of fir and would feel the tinsel strands tickle my nose. I felt at peace, safely guarded by the angel on top. My mother would make cinnamon cookies and hot cocoa and my father would read "A Christmas Carol" out loud every year as I lay there and soaked in the wonders of the season.

Alas, I am now too old to lie on the floor. I can still get down there, but getting up again is difficult. We never use tinsel as it's dangerous for the cats. And our tree, sturdy plastic and aluminum, doesn't smell like Christmas. But there are blessings to the "new" tree as great as my memories of the old.

Because the tree is artificial, we can put it up early and leave it up as long as we want. No needles on the floor or water spilling onto packages.

We put on as many twinkling colored lights as possible. They're LED now instead of the giant ones I had as a kid, so they use less power and hide in the branches to give glimmers of color. We still have an angel on top of the tree – she's not the angel from my childhood, but she's the angel my son will remember from HIS childhood.

My father is gone, and no one reads Scrooge to me anymore. I must read it myself or watch one of the many movie versions. We watch as many holiday movies as time will allow, culminating with "It's a Wonderful Life" on Christmas Eve. We drink cocoa and eat our cookies, even though they're likely to be store bought.

Sometimes I miss the old traditions. I grow nostalgic at this time of year. But I haven't lost the wonder. As I gaze at our tree from the comfort of my recliner, I am still entranced by the sparkles, the colors, and the memories contained in each ornament. The little girl that crawled under the tree still exists. She is carried deep within my heart.

December Week 3:

It's that time of year. The winter holidays are coming so thick and fast, it's hard to keep them straight. From November until January, it's a whirlwind of celebrations!

Hannukah is upon us. The holiday celebrates the Maccabees retaking Jerusalem and rededicating the temple in Jerusalem in the second century BCE. Candles are lit for eight nights with songs and prayers.

Las Posadas (The Inns) is a nine-day festival honors the journey taken by Mary and Joseph as they searched for a Bethlehem inn. Children lead processions through the streets singing and asking for shelter. After, they break pinatas shaped like the star of the wise men.

Some Native American tribes celebrate Soyal, a recognition of the turning of time. There are prayers and feasting, as well as a ceremony to invoke the return of the Sun God from his travels away from the tribes during the winter.

Many people around the world celebrate Christmas, a remembrance of the birth of the Christ Child. We give presents, share time and food with family and friends, and have special prayers and music.

Kwanzaa was created in 1966, after the Watts riots.

There are seven nights, each with its own candle and ceremony. Every night focusses on a different principle: unity, self-determination, collective work/responsibility, cooperative economics, purpose, creativity, and faith.

Then we have New Year's Eve and Day. We celebrate the coming of a new year with fireworks, noise makers, and parties. We make plans for the next year to be better people and to take care of ourselves and our world.

Do you notice a common denominator in all of these holidays? They all celebrate light – candles, the sun, fireworks – they all remind us that there is light in the darkness, that there is still hope.

In one Dr. Who Christmas special, they expressed it like this:

"On every world, wherever people are, in the deepest part of the winter, at the exact mid-point, everybody stops and turns and hugs. As if to say, "Well done. Well done, everyone! We're halfway out of the dark." Back on Earth we call this Christmas. Or the Winter Solstice."

So well done, everyone. We're halfway out of the dark. Happy holidays to all.

December Week 4:

December brings thoughts of endings. The days grow ever shorter, the trees are bare, the year draws to a close. And endings often bring sadness.

And yet, everything passes in its time. The stars burn out, the seasons change, loved ones pass beyond our comprehension. We rarely know when each passing will occur. And we control absolutely none of it.

Endings, as hard as they can seem, are necessary. Barrenness, dormancy, oblivion, provide us with time to rest, to reflect, to remember. Knowing what little time we have should make us more conscious of living for each moment, but it often takes a loss for us to recognize the gifts in our lives.

As we look forward to a new season, to a new experience, to a new life being born into this world, let's not be so quick to ignore the slow, lulling, interval of endings. Let's use them as a reminder of all that we have loved.

Ruminations

January Week 1:

Netflix is a blessing to me.

I know, I know… there are better things to do with my time than sit in front of a TV streaming reruns. But, for me, it's a necessity. If I sit quietly, my brain starts lying to me. It tells me things like, "You're worthless. You are a burden. You don't deserve what you have."

I don't know where I learned these ideas. I don't truly believe them. But my chronic depression added to my chronic anxiety creates these scenarios.

I need distraction.

So I watch TV. Currently, I'm re-watching sitcoms from the 1980s. No violence, drugs, or sex, just life lessons with a touch of humor. I need the humor. I REALLY need the humor. And while my brain is being occupied with Netflix, my hands are busy knitting, quilting, crocheting, or petting the cat. These are the things that bring me joy and make me feel useful.

So if you suffer from lying brain weasels like me, I encourage you. Do whatever works. If it's reading, exercise, prayer, activism, meditation – even watching old reruns – if it works for you, go for it! And don't let anyone tell you that there are better things to occupy your time. You know your body and your soul. You take care of you!

PONDERINGS

January Week 2:

I'm cold. I'm tired. I don't want to. You can't make me.

Sounds like I live with a teenager, doesn't it? But no, it's just my aging, aching body, complaining about getting out of bed. Sometimes I think I could happily spend the rest of my life lying in bed, but that's not very realistic. If nothing else, I'll have to go to the bathroom eventually.

So I haul myself up and pad down the hallway. Morning pills, breakfast, check the email, start a new day. I spend most of my days on the couch. I don't have much energy, so I need to rest a lot. And watching Netflix can get boring (what do you do after you've seen it all???), so I knit or crochet, do some hand sewing, or play games on my phone.

But occasionally, I remember to look out our dining room windows. We have a bird feeder there and a honeysuckle bush that is covered with little finches, sparrows, and other birds we just call LBJs (Little Brown Jobbies). They fight over the feeder, pushing each other off the perch and waiting in line on the fence. My husband fills the feeder every morning and it's always empty by nightfall.

I can also watch the seasons change. Today, the sun is shining and there's a light breeze making the branches bow and shake. The bougainvillea still has some bright pink blossoms in its sheltered corner. The sunlight dapples the stucco walls of the garage, painting pictures in the shadows. The clouds are drifting slowly by, white and fluffy in the afternoon sky.

"Now, see?" I tell myself. "You would have missed all of this if you had stayed in bed." I make a mental note to remember that tomorrow.

January Week 3:

How do you define strength? Can you lift heavy weights? Can you unscrew the tightest jar lids? Can you smile through adversity? Can you help others carry their loads?

I tend to see myself as frail, weak, less than. But actually, I am very strong! Or at least stubborn, which can serve the same purpose. I may not be able to lift heavy weights, but I do something that many people cannot.

I get up every day, get dressed, and set myself a task to accomplish.

I know, that doesn't sound like much, but it is. For me. Some days the task is to clean a room, or fold the laundry, or make a shirt. Other days, I schedule paying the bills, or working on my knitting, or reading a book.

And some days, the task is to just sit and be. This is maybe the hardest task of all.

But I give myself something to accomplish every day. And usually, I manage to do it! And that makes me strong.

While growing up, I often wondered what my adult life would be like. This is not what I had imagined. But it is what I have. And I can choose to stay in bed, stop eating and taking my meds, and let myself quietly slip into oblivion, or I can choose to persist in living the life that I have to the best of my ability.

Yes, sometimes I have to cancel plans. And somedays I cry. And many days I complain. But the strength is not in pretending my life is perfect. The strength is in recognizing the imperfections and adjusting my expectations to reality so that I can continue to live. And who knows, maybe the best of my life is still ahead of me.

"As long as we are persistent in our pursuit of our deepest destiny, we will continue to grow. We cannot choose the day or time when we will fully bloom. It happens in its own time."

— *Denis Waitley*

January Week 4:

There's a band we like that plays in our town occasionally. They're called "Decades" because they play music from the last 50 years – today's hits, old favorites, you name it – they play it.

I was thinking about decades today, the band and the decades of our lives. At 65, I have more life behind me than in front of me, so it's easy to look back at the decades and recognize how they have shaped me.

My teenage years were rough. I had a lot of physical problems and that led to a lot of emotional problems. I made a lot of mistakes. But I survived – and believe me when I tell you I often thought I wouldn't. In fact, there were times when I didn't want to survive. It wasn't easy or fun, but I made it through.

In my 20s, I had my first husband, my first full-time job, and my son. There were ups and downs, learning to negotiate living with someone else, and learning how to get by on no sleep.

My 30s gave me my first college degree, my first divorce, and my first real career. I learned how to be on my own, how to balance my own budget, and how to navigate the workplace. I also gained a second husband and a second divorce.

I was in my 40s when I finally felt like I came into my own. I was financially independent, earned my second college degree, and made good solid career choices. I learned to ice skate and how to wallpaper. I learned what it was like to lose a parent and how to navigate the emotional and practical issues surrounding death.

By the time I was in my 50s, I had bought and sold my first home. I packed up everything I owned and moved across the country to start yet another college degree. Changing career paths, being single and child-free, and trying to fit in with a MUCH younger crowd were all challenges, but I persisted.

My 50s changed me a lot. I had a new career with a new degree. I met the love of my life and married him. I lost my mom. I was diagnosed with cancer and chronic fatigue. I became disabled.

Now I'm smack in the middle of my 60s. And as I look back, I can see the things I learned through each decade; some of it was horrible and some of it was wonderful. So I remember the old favorites, embrace some of the latest hits, and keep adjusting to the changes each decade bring. I am still learning, and I persist.

February Week 1:

When I was young, I remember my grandmother saying that she had grown too old for this world. I thought it was an odd thing to say, but now… I kind of get what she was saying. She was born in 1898 and lived to be 92 years old. Just think about what happened in those years! She went from living in a dirt house carved into a hillside, with no indoor plumbing, to living in a world where the internet and personal computers were taking off.

She also lived in a time when guns were for hunting to feed the family instead of for killing random strangers on the street. And although she couldn't count on the weather being perfect for the crops, she could be sure that winters would be cold and summers would be hot.

She knew her neighbors. Her kids could play outside unattended. She could cook on a woodstove and feed a veritable army of farmhands and kids. She did laundry by hand and was grateful when she got a hand-crank wringer to help.

The world now is a very different place. Sometimes, when I see the homeless and the addicts outside the stores and restaurants, when I read about the floods and fires caused by humanity's hubris, or when I am shocked – not by yet another mass shooting, but by the fact that I am not surprised by it – I, too, feel that

I have grown too old for this world.

But people are funny. They adapt. They continue. I watch my nieces raising their babies, giving them love and hope. They work in hospitals and schools, making a difference to people's lives. Our friends send us notes of love. We share in each other's joys and sorrows. We build, create, nurture, plan, and believe as if tomorrow is assured – that the world will continue.

And so I believe that it will. It must. It will not be the world my grandmother knew. It will not even be the world I grew up in, or that my son grew up in. But it will continue. And the wonderful, crazy, adaptable human race will find a way to live in it. Because they will always plant love, hope, and courage.

February Week 2:

Don't sweat the small stuff.

The Devil is in the details.

Little things mean a lot.

Or, to quote one of my favorite musicals (with thanks to Stephen Sondheim), "If life were made of moments, even now and then a bad one… But if life were made of moments, then you'd never know you had one."

Life is, of course, made of moments. Every day holds myriad little things. But we often look at the big picture instead of noticing the little things.

Spilled my coffee? Boss was grumpy? Traffic was insane? Must be a bad day. We take the small annoyances and project them throughout our entire day. Sometimes, the mood I wake up in sets the tone for everything else that will happen to me that day.

But there are SO MANY moments in a day. They can't all be bad, can they? Hearing a baby laugh (my favorite sound), reading a note from a friend, watching flowers dance in the sunshine – these things all add up to a good day.

Truth be told, most days are a mixture. There are annoyances, aggravations, and irritations. But there are also giggles, gratitude, and generosity.

What kind of day you have is decided by which moments you focus on.

Today was a good day. It's a small victory, but I'll take it!

February Week 3:

"If all of our problems were hung on a line,
  You would choose yours and I would choose
  mine."

Think about the idea. Imagine an old-fashioned clothesline stretching around the world. Everyone is invited to bring their problems out and hang them on the line. Flapping in the breeze, the problems shake off the dust and cobwebs that have accumulated over the years. They shine in the sun, offering change.

Now you can step up and choose a problem or two. You get to choose as many as you hung up, so the number stays the same. Which problems would you choose?

The rich person complaining about how expensive fuel for their yacht has become? The simple soul who is losing their faith? What about the person who has a lousy cold?

I don't know, they sure seem better than my problems. The catch is, to take on another person's problems, you have to become that person. Maybe the rich person is spending frivolously to cover an addiction, or a loss of meaning in their life. Perhaps the person with a cold actually has Covid or lung cancer. Would you really want to become someone else? Can you really imagine yourself is someone else's life? We never truly know what another person may be going through.

It could be true that you are better off with the devil you know than the one you don't. I may whine and complain about my life sometimes, but it's all mine. I own it. I claim it. And the battles I fight are familiar by now. I recognize the first signs of a problem and can adapt to alleviate it.

I don't want someone else's life. I want to make the most out of the life I have.

February Week 4:

Gratitude changes your attitude and your outlook. And it's good to be reminded once in a while of all the blessings in your life. We tend to take so many things for granted – a roof over our heads, food on the table, friends, and family.

But really, look around. The world is in a bit of a mess, don't you think? Wars, famine, disease, and death. These things are always with us. They are not caused by some great overseer, but rather by petty human jealousy and greed.

The world has more scientific and educational resources than ever before in human history, and yet we haven't eradicated these pernicious evils. In fact, they seem to increase with each passing year.

So be grateful for all you have. Sleep soundly, knowing you are safe. Eat well, grateful for the bounty in your life. Laugh with friends and family. But spare a thought for the ones who are without. Work in your own way to make things better for everyone. Spread the blessings as far and as wide as you possibly can.

For what is gratitude without compassion?

Contemplations

Extra Winter Thoughts:

I come from a long line of worriers. The men in my family seem to just float along, taking life as it comes. But the women? We worry about the economy, our children, our loved ones, wars, crime, drugs… you get the idea.

Worry stems from fear. Specifically, fear of the unknown. When we can't see the outcome of a given situation, we create possible outcomes in our heads and, all too often, the possibilities are negative.

For example, let's say I misplace my phone (which happens frequently). No big deal. It has to be somewhere in the house, right? But my brain jumps into hypervigilant overdrive. It goes something like this:

"I can't find my phone. What if someone needs me? My son is off on vacation. What if he's in a car accident? Or arrested? How will he reach me? Or maybe he's fine. But what if I fall? My husband is listening to music and won't hear me yell for him. I could lie here, on the bathroom floor, bleeding from a head wound, slowly growing weaker until I die in a puddle of my own blood, all because I CAN'T FIND MY PHONE!"

It's silly. Rationally, I know none of those scenarios are likely to happen. The outcome will be entirely different, and usually benign. But not all fears are unfounded. As we grow older, we are more likely to rely on family, friends, and caregivers. We try to accept it, but deep down, we may mourn the loss of our energy, our security, and our self-reliance.

I am not in the best of health. I need assistance on a daily basis. And it worries me. My life is carefully bound and supported by the love of the man I married. He is strong and healthy and will probably outlive me. In fact, I made him promise he would outlive me! But the fear that he will die first and I will be left alone is real and altogether possible.

Sometimes, late at night, as he lies sleeping next to me, I am overwhelmed by the magnitude of love he shows me every day. His caring, thoughtful presence is my comfort and my strength. And my greatest fear is that I will have to someday learn to survive without him.

REFLECTIONS

One Final Thought:

"Star light, star bright,
  First star I see tonight,
  Wish I may, wish I might,
  Have the wish I wish tonight."

You know, as often as I said that rhyme throughout my childhood, I don't remember a single wish being granted. But I also don't remember what I wished for. Childhood wishes are ephemeral. They last for a moment and then they're gone.

I still have wishes. But they linger. And I know that the only way they can come true is by working and planning and creating. And I know that I can't make them come true all by myself.

I wish… I wish…
I wish for world peace.
I wish that everyone had enough to eat.
I wish that we could all be healthy.
I wish that everyone knew that they were loved.
I wish that all of humanity could share these wishes.
I wish *you* hope, love, forgiveness, and comfort.

This book would simply not exist without the help and support of the following:

All the various therapists in my past – I learned something from each of you.

Scott 'Q' Marcus – thanks for asking me to share my thoughts on your page.

Lisa Turay – the one who taught me to let go of shame and guilt.

Greg Shepard – for everything you are and do, always and for the rest of my life.